What's Inside?

by Mary Jane Martin

SCHOLASTIC INC.
New York Toronto London Auckland Sydney

COVER: © Alan Blank/Bruce Coleman Inc.

PHOTOGRAPHY CREDITS:
p. 3: © G.I. Bernard/Animals Animals. p. 4: © S.J. Kraseman/Peter Arnold Inc.
p. 5: © E.R. Degginger/Photo Researchers, Inc. p. 6: Zig Leszczynski/Animals Animals.
p. 7: © Laura Riley/Bruce Coleman Inc. p. 8: © Robert W. Hernandez/Photo Researchers Inc.
p. 9: © Dwight Kuhn. p. 10: © Dwight Kuhn. p. 11: © J. H. Robinson/Photo Researchers.
p. 12: © J.H. Robinson/Photo Researchers. p. 13: © C.C. Lockwood/Animals Animals.
p.14: © G.R. Zahm/Bruce Coleman Inc. p. 15: © E.R. Degginger/Animals Animals.
p. 16: E.R. Degginger/Photo Researchers.

Copyright © 1994 by Scholastic Inc.
All rights reserved. Published by Scholastic Inc.
Printed in the U.S.A.
ISBN 0-590-29204-8 (meets NASTA specifications)

7 8 9 10   09   00 99 98 97

What's inside?

It's a baby chicken.
That's what's inside.

What's inside?

It's a baby turtle.
That's what's inside.

What's inside?

It's a baby penguin.
That's what's inside.

What's inside?

It's a baby fish.

That's what's inside.

What's inside?

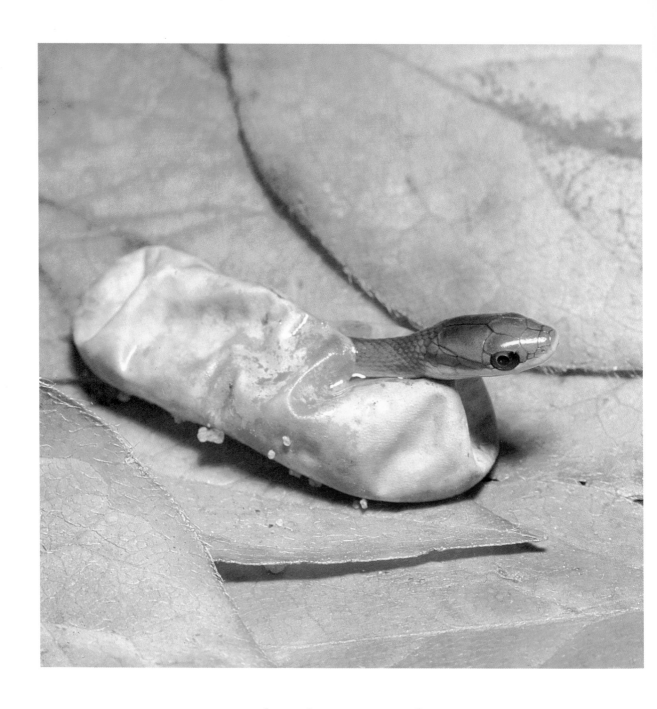

It's a baby snake.

That's what's inside.

What's inside?

It's a baby heron.
That's what's inside.